# All That We Are

Moments, Memories, and the Love That Built Us

Vani Jain

Copyright © 2025 Vani Jain

All Rights Reserved.



Made with ❤ on the Notion Press Platform

www.notionpress.com

*For the ones who built my world*

*before I knew I had one.*

Home

# Contents

# Foreword

In a world where everything moves too fast, this book is a pause. A soft landing. A reminder of the quiet magic we often overlook — the way a mother listens without judgment, a father shows up even when exhausted and a sister becomes both protector and partner in crime.

Vani Jain's *All That We Are* isn't just a collection of poems. It's a living scrapbook — full of laughter, memories, chaos, and comfort. These are the kind of words that make you want to call home, or maybe, just never leave it.

Saanvi Jain

14 May 2025

# Preface

I didn't plan to write a book.
I just started writing down things I didn't want to forget.

The way Mumma nods when she already knows what I'm feeling.
Papa's habit of saying "yes" even before I finish my sentence.
Didi turning into half-sister, half-parent whenever I mess up.
Fudge making the whole house feel alive with just one tail wag.

These pages are full of stuff that felt too small to be remembered…
But too important to ever let go.

It's not perfect. It's not fancy.
But it's *us* — messy, loud, soft, chaotic, and full of love in ways that don't always make sense to others, but always make sense to me.

Vani Jain

14 May 2025

# Acknowledgments

To Mumma —
For the unconditional love, silent strength, and being the heart of our home. You taught me what grace really looks like.

To Papa —
For always picking up the phone, even at 2 a.m. You are my calm, my backup plan, and my first superhero.

To Didi —
You've been my shield, my sass partner, and my forever text-away. Thank you for never letting me spiral alone.

To Dadi, Nanu & Nani —
For the stories, the patience, and the roots that hold me steady.

To Fudge —
You didn't just steal my slippers — you stole our hearts. Thank you for loving us like only you could.

And to *you*, reading this —
If this book reminds you of your people, call them. Or better yet, write to them. It's worth it.

# Introduction

Let's be honest — this isn't a book.
It's a love letter. In pieces. In poems. In memories I wrote
so I wouldn't forget how it all *felt*.

You won't find epic stories or world-changing lessons here.
You'll find hotel room breakfasts, gossip in the car,
midnight lectures, and burnt toast we laughed over anyway.

You'll find people — my people — who've seen every
version of me and still choose to stay.
People who've shown me that home isn't a place or a
moment.
It's them.

So here it is. The book I didn't know I was writing, for the
people who didn't ask for it — but totally deserve it.
A thank you, wrapped in rhyme and realness.

# Our First Home

It isn't a place
we call home.
It is the way you make it ours—
the quiet mornings with no rush,
the late-night talks we didn't know we need.

Home is in the way
you always know when something's off,
even when we don't say a word.
In the way you never leave us feeling alone,
even when you are tired.

It is never the walls that keep us safe,
it is the way you hold it all together,
even when the world is falling apart.

You show us that home
Isn't just a place.
It is always you.

# Jupiter

We've seen deserts, islands, mountaintops.
But the wanderlust didn't stop with Earth.

We've crossed seas,
caught trains,
survived airports and delays.

Sometimes I think about a rocket—
just us.
No strangers. No Wi-Fi. No noise.

Next stop: Jupiter.
Because… why not?

# Passport Pages

UK. Dubai. Spain. The world.
But my favorite destination?
Four tickets. One room. Us.
Jet lagged and laughing in hotel rooms.

Suitcases that carry both clothes and chaos,
And a love that unpacks itself
In every shared selfie, every half-burnt toast.

The places were new, but the feeling familiar —
You made foreign cities feel like home.
With every map we crumpled, every wrong turn we took,
We stitched new memories into old habits.

In that clutter of souvenirs and sunburns,
I learned:
the best place in the world is wherever you are.

# The Gossip Car

Windows down, secrets up,
Somehow, between red lights and left turns,
We told each other more truth
Than any dinner table ever got.

The AC low, our voices high.
Every stoplight a stage, every U-turn a plot twist.
We laughed harder than the horn behind us,
Spilled more tea than our flasks could hold.

# Bringing Fudge Home

We weren't just getting a puppy,
we were welcoming a piece of joy.
One car, four hearts
already falling in love with a bark we hadn't heard yet.

That drive home felt like magic—
our voices softer,
our laughter warmer,
a new life nestled in backseat dreams.

# We Don't Pick Sides

We yell.
Slam doors.
Cry.
But never once have you said,
"She was right."

You've only said,
"Let's fix it together."
And somehow,
that has always been enough.

# Last Minute Love

8

You always say yes
two hours before the mall closes.
Maybe that's what love looks like—
tired, but still walking beside me.

And even when your feet ache
you match my pace,
never rushing me out
of the world I want to linger in.

# The Red Invisible String

I've heard of this invisible string,

A thread that connects us all to everything.

Some say it's fate, some say it's luck,

But when I see the love between you both,

I start to believe in that stuff.


Maybe it's real, maybe it's just a thought,

But watching you two, I'm sure I've caught

A glimpse of that string, strong and bright,

That keeps you together, day and night.

A red invisible string pulling me back to you.

# The Fire Brigades

You both rush in when things catch flame —
Not to scold, not to scream,
But to hold, to cool, to patch the cracks
in two daughters who argue like a wildfire.
And when the smoke clears, it's you we find —
Arms outstretched, laughter ready,
Ready to forgive even what was never said aloud.

In moments loud and loudest still,
You are the silence that steadies us.
In tempers and teacups, in storms and spoiled moods,
It is your calm that folds around us,
A fire brigade not just for flames,
But for feelings too wild to name.

# Inheritance

You gave me more than names and skin,
You handed down the quiet things—
The way to lose, the way to win,
The strength to stand when everything sinks.

You taught me not to chase the light,
But how to spark it from within—
And now, when I am far from home,
I carry you beneath my skin.

# The Mirror Split

They say I'm Dad,
she's Mom —
but really, I see both of you
when I laugh, when I stress,
when I dare to love fully.

In every sharp word,
in every soft gesture,
I carry your echoes,
blended into who I am becoming.

# The Invisible Net

Even when I didn't fall,
You were already below, arms wide.
I never asked for that safety —
But I always knew it was there.
Like breath, like gravity, like background noise,
Your love caught me before I even jumped.

And now when I walk my own line,
Shaky and scared some days,
I still feel that net —
Invisible, unspoken, but always ready.
Not a question, not a maybe —
Just there. Just you.

# The Dream Team

One's the calm, one's the fire,
One holds me close, one lifts me higher.
One's all heart, the other's will,
One says "yes," the other agrees (eventually).

You're my mess-fixers, trip-planners, spies,
Mind readers behind parent disguise.
Together, you're magic — quiet but still

# If Love Had a Recipe

Start with one cup of patience,
Two tablespoons of "I believe in you,"
A generous pour of midnight talks,
And a pinch of "I told you so" (just for flavor).

Fold in the way they look at you when you're lost,
Mix gently with sacrifices never spoken.
Bake through years of showing up,
Even when they're tired, even when you're not kind.

Top it with hugs that don't need reasons,
And serve warm — every single day.
Garnish with the secret ingredient-
Love.

For Papa-

# Coolest of Them All

You walk in like the boss you are —

But when I say "Dad,"

You melt, instantly.


You switch from warrior to softie

In under a second.

That's your magic.

# Daddy's 2 Princesses

He calls us his girls, his pride, his light,

Says we make his every day feel right.

One's the calm, and one's the storm,

But both of us fit in his arms so warm.


From last-minute plans to taking fudge on drives,

To silly talks that light up our lives,

He's the king of saying "yes" with a smile,

Even when we test his peace once in a while.


We've got different moods and matching shoes,

And somehow, he keeps up with our every news.

Two princesses — wild, loud, and blessed,

But to him, we'll always be his very best.

# Life Of The Party

He walks in and suddenly the room's alive,

With jokes and stories that instantly thrive.

Cooler than cool, with effortless flair,

Our dad's got vibes that fill the air.


Music? He'll dance. Silence? He'll joke.

He's the spark in the laughter, never goes broke.

From parties to road trips, he's always the vibe,

Our built-in playlist — the chillest tribe

# Car Chats

Dad and I in the car, just the two of us,

No need for big talks, no need to fuss.

We talk about everything — work, love, and life,

Even the stuff that can stir up some spice.


I smirk a little, and he throws in a pun,

Then we laugh about things I barely outrun.

But that's dad's magic — the moments we share,

In the car, like the world isn't even there.

# You and Mom – The Team

I've seen how you fight — and how you mend,

You're not just her partner, you're her best friend.

You both balance each other's  fire with quiet calm,

Together you're the family's balm.


You two — a team, no drama, all grace,

Sorting chaos with one single face.

You've taught me what love should be,

Through fights and late-night talks.

# The Businessman Who Shows Up

You're running factories, calls back to back,

Always in motion, never off track.

But still, you never miss my game,

A fest, a meltdown, or a wild claim.


You walk in with that "I got this" air,

Like chaos doesn't even dare.

You're tired, I know — though you never show,

How you do it all? I'll never know.

# Our Favourite Code Word —
# "Yes"

"Can I get this?" — I already know,

You'll fake-think, then say "let's go."

From last-minute wishes to giant asks,

You're the king of unplanned tasks.


Never seen a genie, but I've seen you,

Turning "maybe" into dreams come true.

It's wild how you make it all okay,

Like magic wrapped in a working day.


.

# The 2 AM Man

When things go wrong,

It's your number I dial —

Because I know you'll pick up. Always.


You're the emergency plan

No one sees,

But I'd be lost without.

# His Two Eyes

You always say we're your two eyes —

Not one more loved, not one less true.

And we see the world a little clearer

Because we see it through you.


You teach us strength in stillness,

And kindness that doesn't shout.

You give and give, even when tired —

No drama, no fuss, just love.


We are who we are because of you —

Not just the rules, but the way you care.

And if we're your eyes, dear Papa,

We hope we help you see just how rare you are.

# Forever My Hero

You're not perfect, and that's the point,

You've messed up, fixed up, rebuilt the joint.

And in all that, you taught me more,

Than books or schools ever had in store.


You showed me failure isn't shame,

It's just a stop in a bigger game.

And when I thought I broke your trust,

You showed me love that didn't rust.

28

For Mumma-

# Our Secret Gossip Line

You know the tea before the pot boils,

Details, drama, dates — all in your files.

Even my friends know to behave,

'Cause you blacklist faster than a microwave.


You nod like you're neutral, but I see the smirk,

You've got receipts, and you know how to work.

And me? Your partner in all this spice,

Being your daughter? Kinda feels nice.

# Girls' Day Out

It's just the three of us, hand in hand,

Diving into shops, like it's a wonderland.

Trying on dresses, laughing till we ache,

These are the memories I'll never fake.


She says, "This suits you," I roll my eyes,

She makes a face, dramatic sighs.

It's chaos, bags, and coffee,

But girl days with mom? They always fly.

# No One Notices Like You

You remember my weird cravings,

the dates I forget,

the way I scratch my head when I lie.

You remember me.


Not the version I show,

but the one that hides —

and you love that version

just the same.

# The Heart of Our Home

She's the quiet force that keeps us going,

The one who handles it all without showing.

She's the heartbeat in every little chore,

The reason our home always feels like more.


She's the planner, the fixer, the soul,

The strength that keeps us in control.

She's the heart, the hands, the reason we thrive,

The one who makes our family alive.

# The Fashionista

No one beats you when it comes to style,

Even in PJs, you're runway worthwhile.

You taught me heels aren't just shoes,

They're statements. Mood-setters. Life clues.


I borrow your bags, your grace,

Try to copy your 'angry mom' face.

But I'll never have your swag, your air,

Mom, you're a fashion affair.

# Baking Memories

The kitchen hums with laughter and love,

As flour and sugar dance hand in glove.

Mom's the baker, the queen of taste,

And we're her helpers, no time to waste.


Cakes rise in the oven, golden and bright,

The sweet smell filling the room, pure delight.

Didi and I with batter in our hands,

Making memories, like we planned.

# The Family Glue

We bicker, we scream, we lose the plot,

But you? You hold it all like a knot.

Tight but soft, strong but free,

You're what keeps us "we."


You play UN in our sister fights,

Keeping peace with treats and lights.

Somehow, without making a sound,

You hold the house, and all it surround

# The Finder of All Things Lost

We search high and low, in every place,

Turn the room upside down, but it's a race.

"Mom, where's my…?" we all shout,

And she strolls in, without a doubt.


In seconds, she spots it — like magic, she knows,

The missing keys, the phone that just shows.

We wonder, how does she always win?

The Finder of Lost Things, with a knowing grin.

# The Fashion Police

Mom says, "Wear this, trust me, it's cute,"

But I can't shake off my "this isn't my suit!"

Yet, somehow, when I step out the door,

I'm getting compliments I can't ignore.


She says, "I was young too, I know it all,"

And I pretend I'm not listening — classic stall.

But her style wins, and deep down I know,

I'm basically her... just in Gen Z glow.

# My Forever Friend

If love had a name,

I'd spell it: M-O-M.

You are my origin story,

And my soft place to land.


You're the diary I never outgrow,

The laughter I return to.

You're forever — and then some.

For Didi-

# Borrowed Without Asking

Your lipgloss? No clue where it went,

Though I wore it last night — 100% meant.

Your top? "Looks better on me, you agree?"

You roll your eyes but let me be.


I swear I'll return it... eventually,

(After three pics and a lunch, maybe).

But deep down we both really know,

What's mine is yours — it's our sister code.

# Mom 2.0

"You need to study," she says like a pro,

While I'm panicking and losing control.

She's not Mumma, but oh she plays the part,

With to-do lists, lectures, and a worried heart.


She scolds me, then brings me food in bed,

Tucks my chaos in with a hug instead.

She's a sister, yes,

But she acts like she's my mom.

# Long Distance, Same Heart

You're in a different city now,

But distance changes nothing, somehow.

The calls are short, but hearts stay long,

I text "call me" — it's our lifelong song.


From silly reels to "I'm not okay,"

You're just one message away.

Miles can't mute the way you care,

You're still here — just not right here.

# Exam Eve Madness

I'd cry over chapters, fall apart in fear,

And there you were — always near.

You'd roll your eyes, then sit me down,

"Focus, Vani. We don't have time to drown."


You taught me everything the night before,

Even when I said, "I can't take anymore."

You gave me calm in the middle of mess,

You were the reason I passed that test.

# My Human Shield

I messed up — again — and I didn't even think twice.

Ran straight to you, because who else would make it nice?

You didn't even react. Just did that thing

where you roll your eyes and go, "Okay, I'll handle this…
sigh."


You've stood between me and full-on storms,

calmed Mumma down, made it all feel... normal.

You took the blame sometimes — like it was nothing.

Like my mess was just another thing you were used to
fixing.


I don't say it much, but I always knew:

If the world ever turned on me,

you'd be standing next to me.

# You've Seen It All

You've literally seen every version of me.

Crying on the floor, screaming at walls,

panicking over exams, and then acting like I don't care.

And somehow, you've never left.


You didn't need to fix it,

but still just sat there.

You've seen the worst and still stayed.

That's not small. That's everything.

# Makeup 101

Mumma's the one who taught me how to blend,

She'd show me a dab here, a swipe there,

and somehow it always looked perfect.

No drama. No fuss. Just... glowy.


Then there's Didi — the eye queen,

She showed me how to make those lids pop and lean.

Smokey eye? Winged liner?

She made it seem like I could totally pull it off.


Now I'm over here trying to combine both,

Still messing up, but hey, at least I try.

Thanks to you two, I'm lowkey a pro now —

Or at least, I look like one, half the time.

# Coming Home

When you come back, it's like the house comes alive,

Like Mumma's smile gets a little wider,

And the air feels warmer,

Because you bring something that we need.


Papa count the days until you're here,

Because it's never really the same without you.

You fill up every space with your laughter,

And suddenly, everything feels right again.

# The First to Know

When everything's going sideways,

You're the first to get the text.

I send you screenshots like it's no big deal,

You read them, and know exactly what to say  instantly.


Even when we're miles apart,

You get me without the words.

I don't have to explain the mess,

You just know and make it all make sense.

# My Best Friend

You're the one I fight with the most,

And the one I run to, first, no matter what.

From stealing each other's fries to stealing clothes,

We've lived a thousand lives in our own little code.


You've seen every side of me — wild, quiet, low,

Still stayed, still understood, still chose to show.

Not just my sister, my partner-in-crime till the end,

You're my forever constant, my best friend.

52

For Dadi-

# The Bed Time Trick

"Soja jaldi se bhoot ajaye ga"

She'd whisper low, then smile at some.

I'd laugh but still pull up my sheet,

Not ready yet for ghostly feet.


It wasn't fear, it was her game,

Every night, it felt the same.

A scary story, then a hug so tight—

That's how Dadi said goodnight.

# Cycling to the Park

I'd cycle slowly, just ahead,

While Dadi and the maid walked.

They'd follow behind, step by step,

As I pedaled on, taking my time.


Once we reached, we'd take a few rounds,

Walking along, no rush, just sounds.

Sometimes I'd swing, going up so high,

Dadi would watch, with a smile.

56

57

# For Nanu-

# History Time

Nanu tells me of kings and swords,

Of freedom fights and British lords.

I sit and listen, wide-eyed and still,

His voice is soft, but it gives me a thrill.


Not from books, but from his mind,

Old India lives in how he's kind.

He makes the past feel close and near,

And every word I truly hear.

# He Showed Me My Thing

Nanu sat beside me, slow and calm,

Showing me how to code.

"How to open this?" I'd ask, all wild—

He'd smile like I'm his favourite child.


That old computer, those gentle tips,

Led me to keys and logic flips.

He didn't just teach — he gave me a start,

To find the one thing close to my heart.

60

All That We Are

# For Nani-

# Simple and So Beautiful

She never needs makeup or gold,

Yet somehow glows like stories told.

Her saree plain, her steps so slow,

But everywhere she walks feels glow.


No fancy words, no loud display,

Still everyone listens when she prays.

She's beautiful in just being kind,

The softest heart and clearest mind.

# Dupatta Dancer

I'd grab your dupatta, bright and long,

Wrap it tight and hum a song.

Twirling fast across the floor,

Pretending I was on a stage .


You'd just watch with that soft grin,

Like every spin was some big win.

You never stopped me, not one bit,

Just let me dance and laugh.

# For Fudge-

# The Sock Thief of Sector Sofa

Fudge is a criminal —

Wanted in three rooms for sock theft and slipper sabotage.

Caught red-pawed,

Still somehow the judge gave him belly rubs.


He doesn't fetch —

He negotiates.

A treat for a shoe, a cuddle for a chewed-up charger.


And we? We fall for it.

Every. Single. Time.

Because the real crime is

How fast he stole our hearts.

.

# Doorstep Joy

Every time the bell rings,

You're already there —

Tail wagging like a celebration,

Eyes lit up with "I care."


You don't ask where we went,

Or how long we stayed away.

You just leap into our arms,

Like it's the best part of your day.

# Fudge O'Clock

You don't follow clocks or rules,

but somehow, your timing's right.

You show up when we need a smile,

or when nothing else feels light.


It's always Fudge o'clock —

time for cuddles, barks, and play.

Your love doesn't wear a watch,

but it stays, all day.

Vani Jain

# The Last Poem

If you've made it this far,

you already know —

this book isn't just poems.


Every page is a piece of us:

our noise, our hugs, our weird car fights,

midnight baking, exam panics,

the kind of love that doesn't need grand speeches.


I wrote this

because I wanted to gift you

something that feels like home.